THE
WRITER'S
Adventure

THE WRITER'S

Adventure

AN INTERACTIVE
GUIDE FOR
EXPLORING FICTION

SEXTON BURKE

For more resources for writers, visit www.writersdigest.com.

17 16 15 14 13   5 4 3 2 1

Distributed in Canada by Fraser Direct
100 Armstrong Avenue
Georgetown, Ontario, Canada L7G 5S4
Tel: (905) 877-4411

Distributed in the U.K. and Europe by F+W Media International
Brunel House, Newton Abbot, Devon, TQ12 4PU, England
Tel: (+44) 1626-323200, Fax: (+44) 1626-323319
E-mail: postmaster@davidandcharles.co.uk

Distributed in Australia by Capricorn Link
P.O. Box 704, Windsor, NSW 2756 Australia
Tel: (02) 4577-3555

Edited by Rachel Randall
Designed by Terri Woesner
Cover Illustration by Geoff Raker
Production coordinated by Debbie Thomas

DEDICATION

For Sadie Grace, our big new adventure.

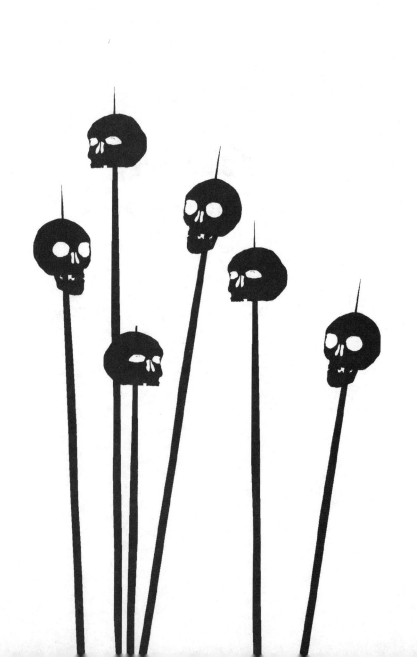

Introduction

Welcome, explorer, to *The Writer's Adventure*!

Strap on your canteen and sheathe that machete—you're about to venture into mysterious places and uncharted realms, and there's likely to be a bit of wildlife to deal with along the way.

But *The Writer's Adventure* isn't just for professionals, no matter how dangerous it may sound. No, this particular quest simply requires that you be willing to try new things, challenge yourself, and enjoy the trip while you're at it. Along the way you'll develop compelling characters and plots, generate unique story ideas, hone your skills, and discover your writing voice. You'll also be charged with exploring every nook and cranny of your creative spirit.

There's no specific path to take or course to chart. You can work your way through the pages one by one or dip in and out as you see fit. The pages are designed to be written or sketched on, colored, torn up—whatever helps you develop those story ideas and explore the writing craft. If you run out of room, feel free to continue your work in a separate journal or on your laptop. The Adventure starts here, but it can end anywhere.

As with any adventure, the bottom line is to have fun and discover new things—and it all starts with a turn of the page.

Good luck!

"Afoot and lighthearted I take to the open road,
healthy, free, the world before me."
—Walt Whitman

Consider the Whitman quote above and think about your approach
to writing. Do you venture into it reluctantly, perhaps with some
trepidation, or do you look forward to every opportunity? Make two
lists below, the first detailing what it is that you love about writing;
the second, everything you struggle with.

Take a moment to examine both lists from the previous page. Do the things you love about writing drive you to write consistently and help you overcome all the negative things that might otherwise hold you back? In the space below, describe in detail what you find to be the single most challenging thing about writing and why it affects you the way it does.

Now determine what needs to be done to overcome this challenge. Don't let yourself believe that you can't do it. All too often, writers allow anxiety, procrastination, boredom, fatigue, and other distractions get in the way of sitting down and producing work. On this page, none of those excuses are allowed. No time to write? Suffering from writer's block? No good ideas? Find a solution. Write it out.

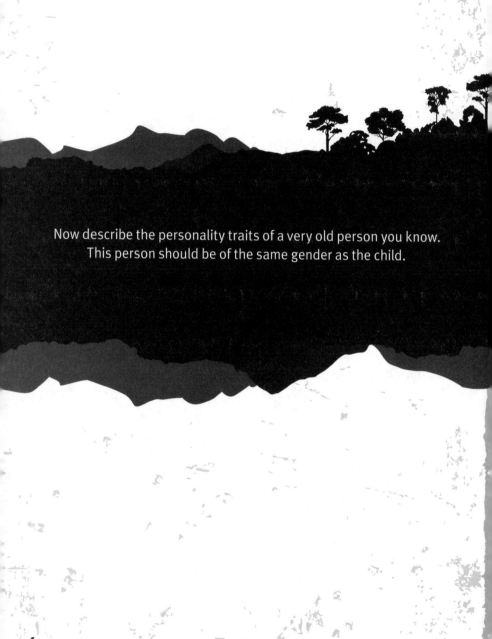

Describe the personality traits of a young child you know.
Be specific and detailed.

Now describe the personality traits of a very old person you know.
This person should be of the same gender as the child.

4

Now make that child a character who grows up to become the older person you've described. In the space below, sketch out a story that explains the changes in the character's personality from young to old.

Think of your favorite children's picture book.
Identify its major theme and write it below.

Now describe the main character's story arc. In other words, what happens to change the status quo of the main character, and what does he do to resolve the change? How is the character changed as a result of this experience?

Now write an original short story meant for adults using the theme and character arc detailed on the previous page.

Remember, strong themes and compelling character arcs are the keys to creating memorable fiction, regardless of genre or audience.

Hugh Hefner once said, "Most of man's great pleasures can be found between a book's covers and beneath a bed's coverlet."

Let's beg to disagree with the second part of that quote. Write a scene in which a character finds something terrifying under the covers.

It takes substantial ego to write and send your words out into the world. It also takes humility to understand that everything you've written can be improved.

Take a look at one of your best stories and rewrite a single scene below. Is there anything you can do to make it better than it is currently? Would the entire piece benefit from another round of revision? Be humble and true in your assessment.

In Greek mythology, the Stygian Witches shared just one eye, meaning only one of them could see at any given time.

Write a scene in which your main character finds herself in a conflict, knowing only a portion of what's happening and why, with any revelations coming intermittently. How does the character handle the situation, and what character traits inform her actions?

11

Pick up a comic book or a graphic novel and flip to a random page. The page is probably broken up into a number of different panels that detail the progression of the story. Select one of the panels and—inspired by the art in this single panel—create a story of your own. Write the opening scene below.

Write down the strongest emotion you've ever felt.
Below that, describe what made you feel that way and why.

In your fiction, have you ever been able to capture a character's emotions so powerfully? If not, try rewriting an extended scene that falls short of powerful, keeping in mind the details that moved you emotionally in real life.

Think of a movie that you like. If you had to associate that movie with a single color, what would it be? For example, you might associate *Lawrence of Arabia* with yellow or brown, or *Midnight in Paris* with red or blue. Next, describe what makes you associate this particular color with the film. Is it physical, emotional, or some other aspect of the piece? Once you've identified your reasoning, use the color as inspiration for an original story of your own. Start writing it below.

Going on an adventure takes courage.
Writing is an adventure.

Stop being humble and acknowledge
that you are courageous.

Some say that bats are nothing more than rats with wings. Assume the opposite is true: that rats are simply bats who lost their wings. Write the story of how this happened.

Great authors often craft fiction that reads like poetry, with each word carefully selected and weighed against those preceding and following it. Take this passage from Clive Barker's novel *Imajica*:

"Perhaps sunlight had always been luminous, and doorways signs of greater passage than that of one room to another. But she'd not noticed it until now."

Take a look at your own writing. Are there moments of poetry in the prose? Write a new scene below and see if thinking about words in this way elevates your writing.

"Not a wasted word. This has been a main point
to my literary thinking all my life."
—Hunter S. Thompson

Using a work in progress, write the next scene you had
in mind below.

Now, using Thompson's quote as your guide, scrutinize that scene for waste and unnecessary words. Can you streamline it, ensuring that every word in the scene has a reason for being there? Do this once below and, if required, try refining it even further on a separate page.

Write a story in which a man is murdered but not killed.

What author do you most admire? Which of his or her books is your favorite? Take a copy of that book and turn to a random page. Close your eyes and put your finger on any line. Open your eyes and write the line down here. Use this as the first line in an original story of your own. As you start writing, pull inspiration from that first line's origins.

Let's call this exercise "Peeling the Onion." Think of a key character that you've created and describe her below. In the outer ring of the "onion" on the opposite page, detail this character's most important trait. Perhaps it's the character's tenacity that enables her to succeed against all odds. Or perhaps she has a fatal flaw.

In the next ring, detail the origins of that trait. What enabled it to develop? Then, in the third ring, describe how those circumstances came about. Finally, in the fourth ring, name the architects behind those circumstances. Follow the trail back as far as you can to determine the history behind the character trait. Use a separate sheet of paper, if needed.

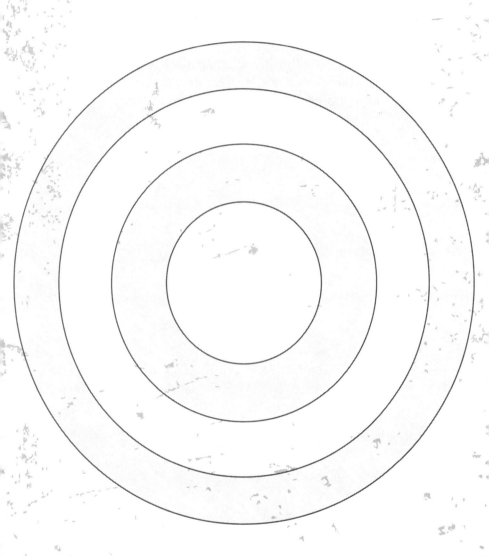

How does this level of understanding about why your character acts the way she does change how you might write her in the future?

In his classic *20 Master Plots*, Ronald B. Tobias describes a quest as "the protagonist's search for a person, place, or thing, tangible or intangible." He also notes that the actual *object* of the quest is ultimately of little importance to the character. What makes the biggest impact is her success or failure in attaining the goal. That's what changes her—not the object itself.

Write a story in which achieving a particular goal means everything to a character. Can you make the story satisfying, even if the character fails in her quest?

Your main character wakes up in the locked trunk of a moving car.
Write the story detailing how this happened and how the story ends.

Your main character works in lower Manhattan. Write a story about a single day in his life—in this case, September 10th, 2001.

The famous philosophical thought-experiment known as the "brain-in-a-vat" argument prompts you to imagine that you're nothing more than a brain in a vat and that everything you experience is due to probes that stimulate various parts of your brain. All that you know is simply an illusion of reality.

Keeping this argument in mind, write a story about someone who discovers that she is nothing more than a brain in a vat. How does this happen, and what does she do about it?

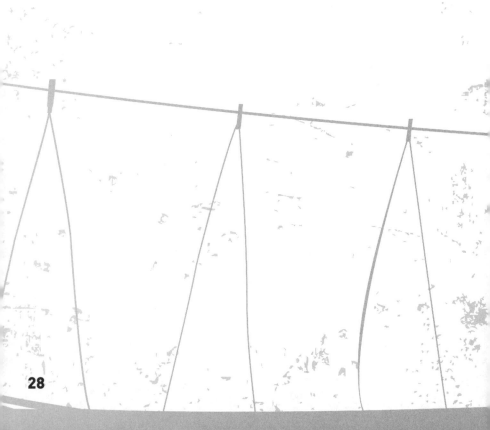

A well-dressed woman sits alone at a table in a very expensive restaurant on a Saturday night. Write her story.

One of the shortest and most famous examples of flash fiction—complete stories told with no more than a few hundred words—is often attributed to Ernest Hemingway. It reads:

For sale: baby shoes, never worn.

Whether or not Hemingway actually penned this story isn't certain, but the words certainly conjure vivid images and emotions just as well as any longer piece of fiction.

Try writing your own piece of micro-flash fiction. Craft a story that is both powerful and subtle using the fewest number of words possible. Can you match or beat "Hemingway's" six?

Rewrite J.M. Barrie's *Peter Pan* as a memoir:
Captain Hook's memoir, specifically.

Sum up your
most important reason for
writing in a single word.

Every time you sit down to write,
put this word at the top of your page.

In the film *A League of Their Own*, Tom Hanks made famous the line, "There's no crying in baseball." It was a criticism of one of his players, but Hanks' delivery of the line imbued it with an undertone of humor rather than cruelty. Can you imbue your own writing with such skillful "delivery" and nuance? Let's find out.

Write a scene in which two arguing characters convey feelings that are at odds with the words they are saying.

Write a short piece in which a blind young woman experiences a brief romantic moment with a passing stranger.

Most writers understand the difference between first-person point of view ("I opened the door, and behind my desk sat the most gorgeous woman I'd ever seen") and third-person point of view ("He opened the door, and behind his desk sat the most gorgeous woman he'd ever seen"), and they know how to write both points of view correctly.

Writing in second person is more challenging as the main character is addressed using second-person personal pronouns ("You opened the door, and behind your desk sat the most gorgeous woman you'd ever seen"), effectively making it seem as if the reader is the main character.

Why not take that idea to the next level? Write a short story in second-person point of view but, at some point in the narrative, make it clear that the reader really has become an active participant in the story.

A jingle is a short phrase, tune, or slogan used to help consumers remember a particular brand or product. For example, nearly everyone remembers Alka-Seltzer's "Plop plop, fizz fizz, oh, what a relief it is" jingle. In ten words, we're told how the product works and what it does for consumers. We're also provided with a unique sound that one can associate with the product.

If you were to write a jingle for your book, what would it be?

If you were to write a jingle representing you, the writer, what would it be?

In Richard Matheson's classic science fiction novel *The Incredible Shrinking Man*, Scott Carey, the protagonist, begins to shrink due to radiation exposure. After many frightening adventures, including a battle with a spider, Carey dwindles to a size so small he can no longer be seen by the naked eye. As he continues to shrink, the book ends with a final thought from Carey: "If nature existed on endless levels, so also might intelligence."

Continue this story. What happens to Carey after he shrinks to microscopic levels and beyond?

Write a story in which your protagonist goes caving with some friends. At some point during the expedition, she gets separated from the party and her light goes out.

Walk through your neighborhood and write down three things you didn't expect to see. When you get back home, write a poem that draws logical connections between those three things.

Think of the thing that's most precious to you. It can be a person, an object, a place, or a state of mind. Write it down below.

Now write a horror story in which your chosen thing is a source of terror.

Your character finds a DVD sitting on the television. The words
"There's no going back..." are written in jagged letters on the top side
of the disc. He pops the DVD into his player and, after watching it,
comes to the realization that the life he knew was a lie all along.

Write the story of what's happened.

H.P. Lovecraft was known for crafting dense narratives that contained very little dialogue and depended upon his mastery of atmosphere and description for their success. Write a story in which no dialogue takes place, but numerous characters interact with one another. Focus on establishing specific moods rather than relationships.

Rewrite the story of Cinderella from
Prince Charming's point of view.

A writer benefits from surrounding herself with honest readers.
Who are yours?

Here's a tough one! One of the limitations of the English language is that all singular third-person pronouns are gender specific except for *it* and *one*. Your options are limited to variations on *he* and *she*, including *him*, *her*, *his*, *hers*, *himself*, and *herself*. This causes problems that you can see reflected in this very book. As the author, I've had to choose either a masculine or feminine pronoun in the process of writing many of the exercises. The only other option would be to use "he or she" in every instance, which is far too cumbersome.

Let's solve the problem. Come up with your own nongender-specific third-person pronoun (and all of its plural, possessive, and objective iterations) and write a story using these words instead of the pronoun goulash noted above.

Do you find that not having to choose one gender pronoun
over another facilitates your writing?

Your phone rings, but you miss the call and no message is left. You Google the number and it comes up as an old boyfriend or girlfriend from high school. Write the story of what happens next.

A well-known verse from Ecclesiastes 1:9 states that:

What has been will be again,
what has been done will be done again;
there is nothing new under the sun.

Write a story in which something truly new—in form, function,
and origin—develops or arrives on planet Earth, and
detail how it might change the world.

Pull a bag of frozen food from your freezer. Hold it against the back of your neck and leave it there for a few seconds. Think about the range of sensations you feel and how those sensations change the longer you leave the item in place. List the sensations below.

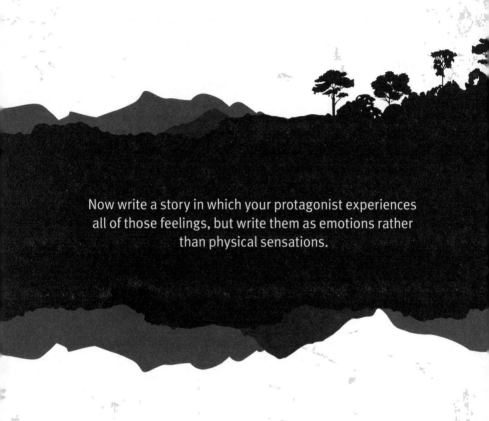

Now write a story in which your protagonist experiences all of those feelings, but write them as emotions rather than physical sensations.

Write a scene in which one character must depart from another.
The first character is overjoyed, while the second is heartbroken.

Indiana Jones is famous for the line, "I don't know, I'm making this up as I go." Be adventurous like Indy. Write a short piece and allow your imagination to go places it normally wouldn't. If you typically write literary fiction, write science fiction. If you write mysteries, write an epic poem. Don't be afraid to get a bit lost.

You will need a six-sided die for this exercise. Randomly select six different items found in your home or office and write them down. Assign each one a number: one through six.

Roll the six-sided die and circle the item on your list that corresponds to the number rolled. Then roll the die again. If one, two, or three comes up, write a scene in which one character tries to seduce another using the object you selected. If four, five, or six comes up, write a scene in which one character tries to kill another using the object in question.

Think of three clichés that you associate with mystery novels. Then pen a short story in which those three clichés are used as the basis for a romance.

In K.T. Tunstall's song "Suddenly I See," the opening lyric states that "Her face is a map of the world, a map of the world. You can see she's a beautiful girl, she's a beautiful girl."

Write a character sketch in which you describe a woman whose face really is "a map of the world." What qualities does this woman have, and how might you use her in a story?

Write a brief history of two characters: how they know one another, whether or not they like one another, and so on. Be specific and detailed.

Now write a scene in which they meet for the first time after ten years, but due to the people surrounding them they can't acknowledge this history. How much of their shared history can you convey through subtext?

A woman traveling with her husband on an American cruise ship suspects one of her fellow passengers of being a terrorist. Unfortunately, she doesn't speak English, and the suspect passenger appears to have vanished. What does she do?

Write a story with the intent of creating something so powerful that someone, somewhere, will claim it must be banned.

Write a scene in which two arguing characters convey feelings that are at odds with the words they are saying.

Write a story from the point of view of someone who's just been diagnosed with Alzheimer's disease.

Select a combination of letters from the name "Arthur Conan Doyle" that form a new word or phrase that represents the key to solving a mystery. For example, "Royal Trade" might be one. Now write the mystery.

Write about a deadly confrontation from the
point of view of a heroic character.

Now write about the same confrontation from the point of view of the antagonist who opposes your first character.

Does he or she have to be a villain?

Write a scene showing the moment when a young man realizes
for the first time that he's in love with his best friend.

In the classic adventure film *The Naked Jungle*, Charlton Heston tries to protect his home from a swarm of army ants. Write a story in which your main character is compelled to protect his home against all odds, even though leaving would be the safest, most suitable thing to do.

Write a story that will move one reader to tears and
another reader to laughter.

Consider what is most precious to you.
Now write a story in which you're offered something
that convinces you to give that thing up.

Choose a famous figure from history and write his or her name below.

Now choose a genre of fiction, and write a short story that puts your chosen historical figure in the genre noted. For example, will Benjamin Franklin fight off a secret alien invasion? Might King Solomon use his great wisdom to solve a murder?

Dracula is an epistolary novel, written as a series of letters, journal entries, and other correspondence. Try your hand at this form. Craft a work of short fiction in which the story is told through a series of documents.

Make up a new word. This word can be a person, place, or thing. Write it on the line below.

_____

Now write a story that convinces readers
this made-up thing is real.

One Halloween a father and his young daughter carve
a jack-o'-lantern. They remove the top of the pumpkin and
reach inside to scoop out the pulp ... only to find something
extraordinary inside. Write a story that explains
what this thing is and how it got there.

Write a story about the day your character finally works up the courage to end an abusive relationship. Keep in mind that just because your character finds the courage doesn't mean he succeeds.

Think of a physical sensation, and write it on the line below.

_____

Now consider the following quote from E.L. Doctorow: "Good writing is supposed to evoke sensation in the reader—not the fact that it is raining, but the feeling of being rained upon."

Write a short piece of fiction in which you evoke the sensation written above. Make the reader feel it.

Write a story that takes place in a not-so-distant future where reading and writing have become things of the past. How do people communicate, and how does the failure to read and write change the way they live, learn, and love?

Through extraordinary circumstances, your protagonist is given the ability to alter reality one time only. What does she decide to do, and what are the ramifications of that decision?

Sit down near two people having a conversation. You might be in a coffee shop, on the bus, or in a doctor's office. Write down any details of the conversation that you're able to hear.

Now write a story based on details from the conversation you overheard.

Write a story in which your main character works in an office. Working late one evening, he makes some copies on the copy machine, but what comes out isn't a copy—it's a message.

Write a story that reveals the truth about the tooth fairy.

Create a character that is kind, intelligent, and wise.

Now write a story that leads to her corruption.

How hard is it to believably corrupt a good person? If it wasn't hard for you to write the prior piece, you should try writing your story again, because it probably wasn't believable either. If it was hard for you, write the story of this character's redemption.

Your protagonist has a "meet-cute" moment with an attractive stranger. In a romance novel or film, this would ultimately lead to love and a relationship. In your story, however, the moment leads to something else. Tell the tale below.

Write a story about someone searching for a lost treasure. Others are seeking this treasure as well. Can you heighten the tension associated with the quest without telling us what the treasure is or why it's important to her?

Above, write down a random paragraph from the worst book you currently have in your home. Below, rewrite that paragraph so it works as the opening of a new story that shows far greater promise than the source of your inspiration.

Create a character whose race is different than your own, then craft a story in which that character's race is the source of either a terrible conflict or a surprising revelation.

Write about a day on Earth from Satan's point of view.

Your protagonist works in New York City, lives a fast-paced lifestyle, and loves it. One day he's offered a juicy promotion with a substantial raise, but only if he moves to a small town in Indiana. Write the story that resolves the conflict.

Put a gun to your character's head.
How did it get there, and what happens next?

Flip through the pages of this book and randomly select one of the stories you've already completed. Now rewrite the same story from the POV of a different character and reveal that not everything is as it originally seemed.

Your protagonist wakes up after a long three-day weekend with an angry bruise on her temple and three spent shell casings in her purse. Unfortunately, she can only remember the first two days. Write the story of her investigation into that missing day.

"Luck is not chance, it's toil;
fortune's expensive smile is earned."
—Emily Dickinson

Are you earning your luck?

Rewrite the story of L. Frank Baum's *The Wonderful Wizard of Oz*, but replace Dorothy with a crotchety old man.

The well-known phrase "tilting at windmills" is derived from a scene found in Cervantes' *Don Quixote*. It's generally used to reference one who fights against nonexistent enemies.

Craft a story in which your protagonist engages in just such a battle.

Write a scene in which at least two characters have a heated conversation that ends in heartbreak.

Now rewrite that scene, but minimize the
amount of dialogue used.

Can you still convey the nature of the conflict, the level of emotion,
and the impact of the final outcome effectively? Is the scene
even stronger for its verbal brevity?

A priest, an electrician, and a duck walk into a bar. But this is no joke. Write the story that brings these three diverse characters together.

Write the story of a character who finds what appear to be drugs, a gun, and an address written on a carefully folded piece of paper in a locked box under her bed.

The Seven Wonders of the Ancient World include the Great Pyramid of Giza in Egypt, the Hanging Gardens of Babylon, the Statue of Zeus at Olympia, the Temple of Artemis at Ephesus, the Mausoleum at Halicarnassus, the Colossus of Rhodes, and the Lighthouse of Alexandria. Only one of these—the Great Pyramid—still stands today. Write a story in which your protagonist learns that this last remaining site holds the key to finding an as-yet undiscovered eighth Wonder.

Your protagonist is a blind woman. She's admitted into an experimental program that enables her to see for the first time. Write the story of that experience.

Write the same story a second time, but in this case
your protagonist is a man.

How does changing the gender of your character
change the nature of the experience?

Write a picture book for children. If it helps to sketch out the pages, do so. Don't worry about the quality of the art, however. Instead focus on the quality of the storytelling.

What happens when it's proven conclusively that the radiation emitted by smartphones does indeed cause cancer—and that the rate of incidence is on the rise?

"Find out what your hero wants. Then just follow him."
—Ray Bradbury

Can writing fiction really be that simple? Rather than thinking up a plot in advance, start with a character. Create someone interesting and write the opening scene that introduces her to the reader. Then introduce a change to the character's status quo that propels her into action.

Was the strength of your character and her desires enough to carry the story from beginning to end without sagging in the middle?

Write a poem designed to terrify the reader. Can you evoke
such strong emotions without using prose?

Write a short story and imbue it with as much conflict and tension as you can. As you approach the climax, complicate matters even further so your hero's situation becomes graver than originally intended.

Was your character able to prevail without relying upon coincidence, deus ex machina, or some other form of lazy storytelling?

Many writers create tension by making the source of that tension obvious: perhaps a looming physical threat or a verbal harangue. On the page below, try using something a bit subtler. Rather than a physical confrontation or other obvious conflict, depend on stillness and quiet to do your dirty work.

Bookstores are typically considered a haven from the rest of the world. Write a story in which a bookstore becomes an outpost from which a small group of people protects itself from an outside threat. Make sure the setting is integral to the story.

Urban explorers are those who venture—often illegally—into man-made structures such as abandoned subway tunnels, condemned buildings, sewers, and other off-limits areas of the city. Write a story of one such adrenaline junkie who takes it just a bit too far.

Write down the name of the most memorable character you've ever read about. What are the traits that make this character so memorable? Are they physical, mental, emotional, or a combination of the three?

Now write down the traits of a lead character that you've created.

Do you find that the traits of your own creation are as compelling and distinct as those of your favorite character? If not, think about what you can do to make him more memorable and real.

Films, by their nature, cannot handle the number of themes, characters, and subplots that novels can. Rewrite the opening of your favorite film in prose form, and see if you can enhance the narrative by adding flesh to the screenplay's bones.

Myths and legends are very often based on actual events, people, or creatures. Write a short story about something that will eventually become legend.

Now write a piece of fiction that takes place long after the "real" events you just wrote about. This time, however, make the legend of those events an important piece of your new story.

Does knowing the reality behind the myth help or hinder your creation of the new piece?

Think of a time in your life when you were at your most helpless. Now write a scene that effectively captures that same sense of impotence and fear.

An old, wealthy family is being torn apart by a new addition to their ranks. Who is this person and why is her presence so damaging to the family? Write the story.

The first chapter in John Green's novel *Paper Towns* begins
with the following line:

"The longest day of my life began tardily."

It's a short line, but it stands out for its unusual use of the adverb
tardily. Writers are often told to avoid using adverbs, and yet in this
case the adverb catches our attention and suggests something about
how our protagonist thinks. What better way to begin a story?

Begin a new story below, and take special care to craft a memorable
opening sentence. It doesn't have to be showy or overly descriptive or
begin with a gunfight in order to get a reader's attention. By the same
token, don't be afraid to break some rules to keep a reader intrigued.
Once you've used that first line to establish a tone for the piece, take
the same amount of care writing each line thereafter.

Write a story about a vampire. But this vampire isn't powerful or sexy or evil. In fact, this vampire doesn't even realize he is one ... yet.

H.P. Lovecraft was known for writing "cosmic horror" in which mankind was under constant assault from beings that were beyond both our imagining and the confines of our space and time. Most of Lovecraft's protagonists die or go mad in their efforts to stop these beings from beyond.

Write a Lovecraft-style story in which the nature of the threat is so vast and strange that victory against it depends upon making the ultimate sacrifice.

Write a twenty-six-word poem. Each word should begin with a different letter of the alphabet.

Now write a new poem by rearranging the words used in your original poem. You cannot add, remove, or alter any words.

Write a piece of fiction in which your protagonist is
an unreliable narrator.

In the book *Symbols Images Codes*, author Pamela Jaye Smith states that when a character makes a leap in a film, it's often meant to symbolize "a shift into a different state of being." Given that you're taking part in *The Writer's Adventure*, let's look at the film *Indiana Jones and the Last Crusade* for a good example. In that movie, Indiana Jones has to take a literal leap of faith across an enormous pit in order to save his father. To do so, he needs to let go of his reason and cynicism and embrace faith in a higher power. He covers his heart with his hand, closes his eyes, and simply steps off into the void.

Write a scene in which your own character must make a literal leap that indicates some sort of emotional or intellectual transition. It need not be quite as obvious as Indy's leap, but it should be equally as life altering.

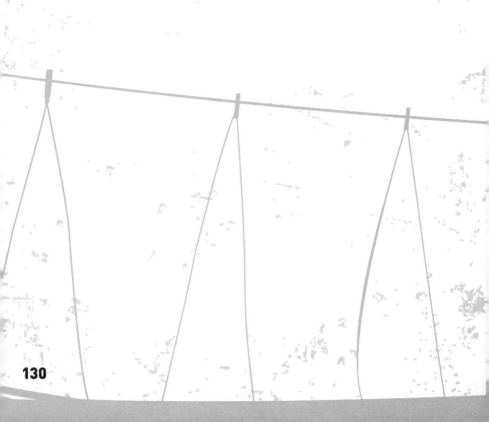

Consider a novel or short story you've already written. Whether it's published or not, write a review of the story below, just as if you were a reader who had to purchase it first. Be objective, truthful, and constructive.

Did you note anything in this review that you could use to improve the work?

The primary convention of most contemporary romantic fiction is that the protagonist and her romantic interest end up together, deeply in love and committed to one another, at the end of the piece . Write a story in which that convention goes unfulfilled.

Can it still be a satisfying romance?

Most works of high fantasy (think *The Lord of the Rings*, The Wheel of Time series, A Song of Ice and Fire, The Earthsea series, and others) are written in third-person point of view, and to a large degree that's due to all the world building that must take place. World building is difficult to accomplish in a first-person narrative because exposition often requires the protagonist to either break character or give a lecture. Still, first-person POV in high fantasy is worth exploring simply because it's done so rarely. Give it a try below.

Write a piece of fiction that has social relevance
and argues for a particular side of an issue. Do so, however,
without naming the issue in question.

Enough exploring for now. Get to work on that story you've been dying to finish.

Write a story in which your bedridden protagonist learns from her doctor that she has only a few days to live. What does she do in the time she has left?

Think of the best story you've ever written. What does the movie trailer for this story look like? Describe it.

In *The Ultimate Secrets of Total Self-Confidence*, Dr. Robert Anthony notes that "psychological studies in personal performance show that individuals who have a plan and goals for their lives are happier and more successful than those who do not."

What are your goals as a writer? Do you have a plan for achieving them—not just the intention for achieving them, but an actual plan? If you do, write your plan below. If you do not, it's time to create one. Write it below.

Write an epilogue to a novel that hasn't been written yet.

Was your epilogue intriguing enough to inspire you to write the actual novel it's meant for?

Write a short essay about the first meal you recall eating as a child.

Take a look at the crossword puzzle in today's paper. If it's not already filled in, complete it before proceeding to the instructions below.

Now write a story that establishes a connection between the answers to 16 across, 3 down, 31 across, and 27 down.

"God only exhibits his thunder and lightning at intervals, and so they always command attention. These are God's adjectives. You thunder and lightning too much; the reader ceases to get under the bed, by and by."
—Mark Twain

Twain's quote on writing is a great one and applies to more than just adjectives. Think about your own writing and how often you try to command the reader's attention with bold action, impressive set pieces, and fiery confrontations. Compare these scenes to your quieter moments. Does the big and bold overpower the insightful and illuminating?

Some novels are built almost entirely on action set pieces, which end up working against the author's intentions of keeping the reader engaged.

Write a short story that balances action with character moments to help ensure reader interest.

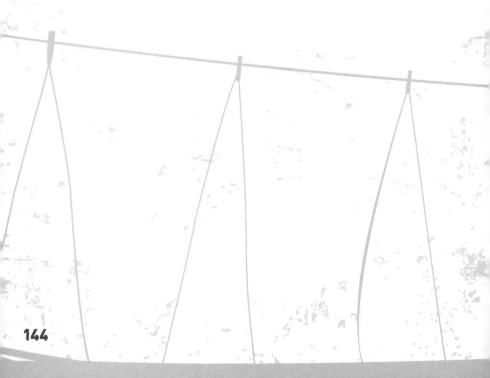

Spoiler Alert! If you're not familiar with *Psycho* (either the book or film), consider skipping this exercise. Fair warning.

In both versions, protagonist Mary Crane is killed halfway through the plot. Though this particular twist is now considered a classic example of bold storytelling, it's not something a writer can get away with often because it so clearly runs counter to "acceptable" conventions of fiction. That said, let's be bold.

Write a story in which a major plot twist—one that changes how readers perceive what's happening—occurs midway through your story.

Think of a place you've never been to but always dreamed of visiting. Now write a story in which you actually travel to this place in your dreams.

The phrase "every dog has its day" was first coined (in a somewhat less contemporary form) by Queen Elizabeth I in the mid-1500s and used by Shakespeare fifty years later in *Hamlet*:

Let Hercules himself do what he may,
The cat will mew and dog will have his day.

Clearly there's some history to this phrase. That being the case, write a piece of historical fiction in which your protagonist finally has her day.

Story ideas are like seeds. There are plenty of them, but they take careful tending to grow into anything worthwhile.

The subgenre of "men's adventure fiction" (including Don Pendleton's Mack Bolan Executioner series and Warren Murphy and Richard Sapir's *The Destroyer*, among others) tends to involve a lot of guns, explosions, and hand-to-hand combat. Write a piece of manly adventure fiction, but break from convention by crafting a climax that depends more on dialogue than destruction. Keep your reader in mind, however. The conversation needs to be as hard edged, riveting, and forceful as any physical conflict.

What happens when a magician discovers that behind all of her stage illusions and sleight of hand, something supernatural—and sinister—is at work?

"I like to listen. I have learned a great deal from listening carefully. Most people never listen."
—Ernest Hemingway

Consider Hemingway's quote, and then write a story in first-person point of view about a character who listens to what is happening but declines to actively participate. At some point in the narrative, he makes a statement that changes every other character's perception of what's really going on.

In Jacques Futrelle's classic short story "The Problem of Cell 13," the protagonist figures out how to escape from a highly secure prison using only his wits and the assistance of an accomplice on the outside.

Write a short story in which your protagonist has the opposite goal: finding a way into a highly secure prison without anyone knowing about it. How would he do this, and why?

Create a superhero. Now write a short story that provides the character with an origin, a motivation, and an archenemy. The challenge? Write it as literary fiction rather than superhero fantasy.

Select a poet from the following list:

Emily Dickinson
Edgar Allan Poe
William Shakespeare
Henry David Thoreau
Walt Whitman
Seamus Heaney

Create the title of a new poem by making an anagram out of the name you selected. Write it down below, and then write the poem inspired by this title.

For example, you might turn "Edgar Allan Poe" into "God, a Lean Pearl."

Animism is the belief that every object, animal, and plant has its own spirit. Write a story in which your protagonist discovers this belief to be an actual fact. How does the character discover it, and what are the ramifications?

In many of his most popular works, Spanish author Arturo Pérez-Reverte combines completely unrelated, heavily researched subjects to construct masterful literary thrillers. In *The Flanders Panel*, the subjects are chess and fine art. In *The Club Dumas*, the subjects are devil worship and antiquarian bookselling (and Alexandre Dumas novels in particular).

Write a thriller that hinges on two unrelated topics about which you are both knowledgable and passionate. The resolution to your thriller depends on working out the connection between the two.

Look through your most recent attempt at writing a novel. With as much objectivity as possible, pick out the least interesting chapter. Rewrite it below, revising as much as needed to make it the most intriguing chapter in the book.

Write the story of a woman living a lie.

In the classic *Grendel* by John Gardner, Grendel details the encounter with Beowulf from his point of view. Consider your favorite piece of classic literature and retell the story from the point of view of either the antagonist or a secondary character.

Pull a book off your shelf and turn to any page. Pick out any sentence, and write down the first four words. Use the first two, three, or four words to create the title of a new story. Here's an example:

Book selected: *Ender's Game*
Page selected: 159
Sentence selected (first four words only): From now on, you

From this sentence I might use any of the following as the title for my new story:

From Now
From Now On
From Now On, You

Try it for yourself, and then use your preferred title as inspiration for the story. Write both the title and the story below.

Grab a copy of your favorite magazine and take a look at the first ad you come across that displays a "scene" with "characters." It might be an ad for perfume, scotch, shoes—anything really. Now write a short story detailing what's happening to the characters. Use the details within the setting of the ad to inform your story.

Write a story about a character who is much wittier than you think you are. What are the traits she displays that indicate this unusually high level of wit?

Your main protagonist has been unable to sleep for several days. Write a story that makes it clear why, and show how sleep deprivation affects your character.

Think of the dullest industry or job you can imagine. Now write a piece of thriller fiction that takes place in this world.

Imagine a day when world leaders come to the realization that human beings—like any other animal species whose rate of population growth negatively impacts the environment—need to be "thinned out." Write a story from the point of view of one of the observers of this decision-making process.

Now write a story from the point of view of a regular citizen.
Under what circumstances do they find out about it,
and what happens next?

In George C. Chesbro's classic mystery series starring Dr. Robert "Mongo" Frederickson, Mongo is an ex-circus acrobat turned private eye. He also happens to be a dwarf. Chesbro never suggests that Mongo's physical condition limits him or makes him less of a PI. In fact, Mongo is perhaps a better PI because of his condition.

Write a story in which your character suffers from a physical disability of some sort, but the nature of that disability actually makes her better at what she does rather than worse.

While visiting the library, your protagonist finds an amusing book on treasure hunting. More intriguing, however, are the obscure clues written in the margins that detail the location of a lost cache of stolen gold. Write the story of this new treasure hunt.

Choose a point in time when an event of historical significance occurred. Now consider how history would have played out had that significant incident never taken place. Write the story.

Think of the most iconic characters in literature. A few examples might include Sherlock Holmes, Katniss Everdeen, James Bond, Jane Eyre, Hannibal Lecter, or Harry Potter. What distinguishes these characters from the thousands of others whose stories are published in any given year? Make a list of the qualities that come to mind below.

Now create an original character of your own. Aspire to create someone who might be just as memorable as any of those noted above. Does your character share some of the same qualities?

Now that you've finished creating your new character, start writing a story using him as either the protagonist or antagonist.

H. Rider Haggard wrote his classic adventure novel *King Solomon's Mines* in order to win a bet with his brother. The wager? Write a novel as good as Robert Louis Stevenson's *Treasure Island*.

Now you take the bet. Try writing a rollicking story of adventure that can stand toe-to-toe with both of these masterworks.

Do you find that giving yourself permission to just have fun—while still trying to achieve a specific goal—enabled you to write faster and with more enthusiasm? If so, how might you apply this lesson to your other writing efforts?

Write a mystery in which two detectives suspect
each other of perpetrating a heinous crime.

Write a scene in which one character tries to seduce
another—but not for the obvious goal of sex.

Write a story about a character who "hits rock bottom." What is this like, and how does your character respond? Is redemption possible, or does your character channel her sorrow into something worse?

Try your hand at writing a piece of prescriptive nonfiction on the topic of writing. Use this as an opportunity to explore what you know about the craft. Focus on what you're best at.

In *Songwriting Without Boundaries*, author Pat Pattison states:

"Finding your voice as a writer is a lot like finding your voice as a singer. If you can carry a tune, you can learn to do it better. You can find, by exploration, where your voice feels strongest, where it feels the most like you. You try different styles, different timbres, different approaches, and, slowly for some, more quickly for others, the real you emerges. The feeling you get when you hit that bull's-eye is like no other feeling. You're incredibly alive and centered, like you've pushed your roots deep into the earth's core. But committing a journey to find that unique voice takes work; it takes practice."

You've been asked to do a lot of exploring—and practicing—in this book. Write down what you've discovered about where your voice feels strongest. Where does it feel most like you? Write about where your journey as a writer goes from here.

Write an epilogue to the story of your life.

About the Author

Sexton Burke is a writer and publisher. He is the author of *The Writer's Lab* as well as numerous other books and magazine articles on the craft of writing. He is also a frequent speaker at writing conferences across the country. Burke currently lives with his wife and daughter in Hoboken, New Jersey, where he works on his fiction whenever possible.

Also Available

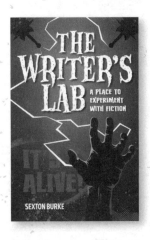

The Writer's Lab is a place in which you can experiment, have fun, and play with prose. There are no rules here—only intriguing prompts and thought-provoking questions. You'll also find plenty of room for writing, planning, and exploring stories.

It's a pure creative outlet through which you'll not only test the boundaries of your ingenuity but learn something about the craft as well.

Rediscover the joy of writing for fun. Experiment with the written word. Take your imagination in entirely new directions.

It's your Lab—use it to create whatever your heart desires.